SCHIRMER'S LIBRARY OF MUSICAL CLASSICS

FREDERIC CHOPIN

Complete Works for the Piano

Edited and Fingered,
and provided with an Introductory Note by

CARL MIKULI

Historical and Analytical Comments by

JAMES HUNEKER

G. SCHIRMER, Inc.

DISTRIBUTED BY

HAL•LEONARD® CORPORATION
7777 W. BLUEMOUND RD. P.O. BOX 13819 MILWAUKEE, WI 53213

FRÉDÉRIC FRANÇOIS CHOPIN

According to a tradition—and, be it said, an erroneous one—Chopin's playing was like that of one dreaming rather than awake—scarcely audible in its continual *pianissimos* and *una cordas*, with feebly developed technique and quite lacking in confidence, or at least indistinct, and distorted out of all rhythmic form by an incessant *tempo rubato!* The effect of these notions could not be otherwise than very prejudicial to the interpretation of his works, even by the most able artists—in their very striving after truthfulness; besides, they are easily accounted for.

Chopin played rarely and always unwillingly in public; "exhibitions" of himself were totally repugnant to his nature. Long years of sickliness and nervous irritability did not always permit him the necessary repose, in the concert-hall, for displaying untrammeled the full wealth of his resources. In more familiar circles, too, he seldom played anything but his shorter pieces, or occasional fragments from the larger works. Small wonder, therefore, that Chopin the Pianist should fail of general recognition.

Yet Chopin possessed a highly developed technique, giving him complete mastery over the instrument. In all styles of touch the evenness of his scales and passages was unsurpassed—nay, fabulous; under his hands the pianoforte needed to envy neither the violin for its bow nor wind-instruments for the living breath. The tones melted one into the other with the liquid effect of beautiful song.

A genuine piano-hand, extremely flexible though not large, enabled him to play arpeggios of most widely dispersed harmonies and passages in wide stretches, which he brought into vogue as something never attempted before; and everything without the slightest apparent exertion, a pleasing freedom and lightness being a distinguishing characteristic of his style. At the same time, the tone which he could *draw out* of the instrument was prodigious, especially in the *cantabiles;* in this regard John Field alone could compare with him.

A lofty, virile energy lent imposing effect to suitable passages—an energy without roughness; on the other hand, he could carry away his hearers by the tenderness of his soulful delivery—a tenderness without affectation. But with all the warmth of his peculiarly ardent temperament, his playing was always within bounds, chaste, polished and at times even severely reserved.

In keeping time Chopin was inflexible, and many will be surprised to learn that the metronome never left his piano. Even in his oft-decried *tempo rubato* one hand—that having the accompaniment—always played on in strict time, while the other, singing the melody, either hesitating as if undecided, or, with increased animation, anticipating with a kind of impatient vehemence as if in passionate utterances, maintained the freedom of musical expression from the fetters of strict regularity.

Some information concerning Chopin the Teacher, even in the shape of a mere sketch, can hardly fail to interest many readers.

Far from regarding his work as a teacher, which his position as an artist and his social connections in Paris rendered difficult of avoidance, as a burdensome task, Chopin daily devoted his entire energies to it for several hours and with genuine delight. True, his demands on the talent and industry of the pupil were very great. There were often "de leçons orageuses" ("stormy lessons"), as they were called in school parlance, and many a fair eye wet with tears departed from the high altar of the Cité d'Orleans, rue St. Lazare, yet without the slightest resentment on that score against the dearly beloved master. For this same severity, so little prone to easy satisfaction, this feverish vehemence with which the master strove to raise his disciples to his own plane, this insistence on the repetition of a passage until it was understood, were a guaranty that he had the pupil's progress at heart. He would glow with a sacred zeal for art; every word from his lips was stimulating and inspiring. Single lessons often lasted literally for several hours in succession, until master and pupil were overcome by fatigue.

On beginning with a pupil, Chopin was chiefly anxious to do away with any stiffness in, or cramped, convulsive movement of, the hand, thereby obtaining the first requisite of a fine technique, "souplesse" (suppleness), and at the same time independence in the motion of the fingers. He was never tired of inculcating that such technical exercises are not merely mechanical, but claim the intelligence and entire will-power of the pupil; and, consequently, that a twentyfold or fortyfold repetition (still the lauded arcanum of so many schools) does no good whatever—not to mention the kind of practising advocated by Kalkbrenner, during which one may also occupy oneself with reading! He treated the various styles of touch very thoroughly, more especially the full-toned *legato.*

As gymnastic aids he recommended bending the wrist inward and outward, the repeated wrist-stroke, the pressing apart of the fingers—but all with an earnest warning against over-exertion. For scale-practice he required a very full tone, as *legato* as possible, at first very slowly and taking a quicker tempo only step by step, and playing with metronomic evenness. To facilitate the passing under of the thumb and passing over of the fingers, the hand was to be bent inward. The scales having many black keys (B major, F-sharp, D-flat) were studied first, C major, as the hardest, coming last. In like order he took up Clementi's Preludes and Exercises, a work which he highly valued on account of its utility. According to Chopin, evenness in scale-playing and arpeggios depends not only on the equality in the strength of the fingers obtained through five-finger exercises, and a perfect freedom of the thumb in passing under and over, but foremostly on the perfectly smooth and constant sideways movement of the hand (not *step* by *step*), letting the elbow hang down freely and loosely at all times. This movement he exemplified by a *glissando* across the keys. After this he gave as studies a selection from Cramer's Études, Clementi's Gradus ad Parnassum, The Finishing Studies in Style by Moscheles, which were very congenial to him, Bach's English and French Suites, and some Preludes and Fugues from the Well-Tempered Clavichord.

Field's and his own nocturnes also figured to a certain extent as studies, for through them—partly by learning from his explanations, partly by hearing and imitating them as played indefatigably by Chopin himself—the pupil was taught to recognize, love and produce the *legato* and the beautiful connected singing tone. For paired notes and chords he exacted strictly simultaneous striking of the notes, an arpeggio being permitted only where marked by the composer himself; in the trill, which he generally commenced on the auxiliary, he required perfect evenness rather than great rapidity, the closing turn to be played easily and without haste.

For the turn (*gruppetto*) and appoggiatura he recommended the great Italian singers as models; he desired octaves to be played with the wrist-stroke, but without losing in fullness of tone thereby. Only far-advanced pupils were given his Études Op. 10 and Op. 25.

Chopin's attention was always directed to teaching correct phrasing. With reference to wrong phrasing he often repeated the apt remark, that it struck him as if some one were reciting, in a language not understood by the speaker, a speech carefully learned by rote, in the course of which the speaker not only neglected the natural quantity of the syllables, but even stopped in the middle of words. The pseudo-musician, he said, shows in a similar way, by his wrong phrasing, that music is not his mother-tongue, but something foreign and incomprehensible to him, and must, like the aforesaid speaker, quite renounce the idea of making any effect upon his hearers by his delivery.

In marking the fingering, especially that peculiar to himself, Chopin was not sparing. Piano-playing owes him many innovations in this respect, whose practicalness caused their speedy adoption, though at first certain authorities, like Kalkbrenner, were fairly horrified by them. For example, Chopin did not hesitate to use the thumb on the black keys, or to pass it under the little finger (with a decided inward bend of the wrist, to be sure), where it facilitated the execution, rendering the latter quieter and smoother. With one and the same finger he often struck two neighboring keys in succession (and this not simply in a slide from a black key to the next white one), without the slightest noticeable break in the continuity of the tones. He frequently passed the longest fingers over each other without the intervention of the thumb (see Étude No. 2, O. 10), and not only in passages where (e.g.) it was made necessary by the holding down of a key with the thumb. The fingering for chromatic thirds based on this device (and marked by himself in Étude No. 5, Op. 25), renders it far easier to obtain the smoothest *legato* in the most rapid tempo, and with a perfectly quiet hand, than the fingering followed before. The fingerings in the present edition are, in most cases, those indicated by Chopin himself; where this is not the case, they are at least marked in conformity with his principles, and therefore calculated to facilitate the execution in accordance with his conceptions.

In the shading he insisted on a real and carefully graduated *crescendo* and *decrescendo*. On phrasing, and on style in general, he gave his pupils invaluable and highly suggestive hints and instructions, assuring himself, however, that they were understood by playing not only single passages, but whole pieces, over and over again, and this with a scrupulous care, an enthusiasm, such as none of his auditors in the concert-hall ever had an opportunity to witness. The whole lesson-hour often passed without the pupil's having played more than a few measures, while Chopin, at a Pleyel upright piano (the pupil always played on a fine concert grand and was obliged to promise to practise on only the best instruments), continually interrupting and correcting, proffered for his admiration and imitation the warm, living ideal of perfect beauty. It may be asserted, without exaggeration, that only the pupil knew Chopin the Pianist in his entire unrivalled greatness.

Chopin most urgently recommended ensemble-playing, the cultivation of the best chamber-music—but only in association with the finest musicians. In case no such opportunity offered, the best substitute would be found in four-hand playing.

With equal insistence he advised his pupils to take up thorough theoretical studies as early as practicable. Whatever their condition in life, the master's great heart always beat warmly for the pupils. A sympathetic, fatherly friend, he inspired them to unwearying endeavor, took unaffected delight in their progress, and at all times had an encouraging word for the wavering and dispirited.

CARL MIKULI.

THE ÉTUDES

I

THE Etudes of Chopin are not only the foundation of his technical system—a system new to pianism when they appeared—but they also comprise some of his most imaginative and enchanting creations, judged exclusively from the musical point of view. Therefore it behooves us to make a somewhat extended investigation of their origins, though for obvious reasons not a comparative critical estimate of various editions. I say "for obvious reasons" because this present edition is definitive and, while adhering to the purity of the original Chopin text, avoids the numerous errors of preceding editions. Suffice it to say that the first complete edition of the Chopin works was Gebethner & Wolff's, of Warsaw; Karasowski gives the date of publication as 1846. Since then, the deluge: Tellefsen, Klindworth, Scholtz, Mikuli, Kahnt, Schuberth, Steingräber—Mertke—Schlesinger (edited by Theodor Kullak), Reinecke, Xaver Scharwenka, von Bülow, D.. Hugo Riemann—the Études and a few of the Preludes—and Hermann Scholtz. Fontana, Wolff, Gutmann, Mikuli, Tellefsen, Mathias, pupils of Chopin, copied from the original manuscripts, and yet they cannot agree, not only as to phrasing and various *tempi*, but even as to the integrity of the text. The errors of certain editions are notorious, nor have modern editions mended matters. By universal assent Mikuli's edition has been pronounced the least defective; yet it leaves much to be desired. In following the Études I shall avoid too many comparisons, for in that case the student would not be able to see the forest because of the trees; above all, no mention of metronome marks, as the action of the modern pianoforte greatly differs from the Pleyel of Chopin's days; the *tempi* then would be old-fashioned now.

Frédéric Chopin, aged twenty, wrote in Warsaw on October 20, 1829, to his friend, Titus Woyciechowski: "I have composed a Study in my own manner"; and in November 14th the same year: "I have written some Studies; in your presence I should play them well." Thus quite modestly did the Polish composer announce an event that proved to be of supreme importance to the piano-playing world. Niecks thinks these Studies were published in the Summer of 1833, July or August, and were numbered opus 10. Another set of Studies, opus 25, did not find a publisher till 1837, though a number of them were composed at the same time as the previous work. A Polish musician who visited the French capital in 1834 heard Chopin play the Studies contained in opus 25. The C minor Study, opus 10, No. 12, commonly known as the "Revolutionary," was born at Stuttgart, September, 1831,"while under the excitement caused by the news of the taking of Warsaw by the Russians, on September 8th, 1831." These dates are given so as to dispel the suspicion that Liszt had influenced Chopin in the production of these masterpieces. In her exhaustive biography of Liszt, Lina Ramann declares that Nos. 9 and 12 of opus 10, and Nos. 11 and 12 of opus 25, reveal the influence of the Hungarian virtuoso. But figures prove the fallacy of her assertion. The influence was in the other direction, as Liszt's three Concert Studies show—not to mention other of his compositions. When Chopin arrived at Paris his style was formed, he was the creator of a new piano technique. The Studies, known as Trois Nouvelles Études, which appeared in 1840 in the Moscheles and Fétis Method of Methods, were afterward separately published. We do not know their date of composition. The manuscript was given to the Princess M. Czartoryska by the composer's sister after his death. The Chopin Studies are poems fit for Parnassus, yet they also serve a very useful purpose in pedagogy. The poetry and passion of the Ballades and Scherzi wind throughout these technical problems like a flaming skein. Both aspects, the material and spiritual, should not be overlooked.

In the first Study of the first book, opus 10, dedicated to Liszt, Chopin at a leap reached new land. Extended chords had been sparingly used by Hummel and Clementi, but to take a dispersed harmony and transform it into an epical Study, to raise the chord of the tenth to heroic stature—only Chopin could have accomplished such a miracle. This first Study in C Major is veritably heroic. The irregular black ascending and descending staircases of notes give the neophyte giddiness. Like the marvellous architectural dreams of Piranesi, these dizzy acclivities and descents of Chopin exercise a hypnotic charm on eye as well as ear. Here in all its nakedness is the new technique; new in the sense of figure, pattern, web, new in a harmonic way. The old order was horrified at the modulatory harshness, the younger generation fascinated and also a trifle frightened. A man who could thus explode a mine that assailed the stars must be reckoned with. The nub of modern piano music is in this study, the most formally reckless ever penned by Chopin. Von Bülow rightfully inveighed against the pervading disposition to play the octave basses arpeggiated; in fact these basses are the argument of the play; they should be granitic, ponderable, powerful. This Study suggests that its composer wished to begin the exposition of his technical system with a skeletonized statement. It is the tree stripped of its bark, the flower of its leaves, yet austere as is the result there are compensating dignity, unswerving logic. With this Study he unlocked, not his heart, but the kingdom of technique. It might for variety's sake be played in unison.

Von Bülow writes that as the second Study in A minor is chromatically related to the Moscheles Étude, opus 70, No. 3, that piece could be used to pave the way for the more musical composition of the Pole. In different degrees of *tempi*, dynamics and rhythmic accent it should be practised, omitting the thumb and first finger. The entire composition, with its murmuring, meandering, chromatic character, is a forerunner to the whispering, weaving, moonlit effects in some of the later Studies. In the third Study we get the intimate Chopin. Its key is E major and it is among the finest flowering of his garden; it is simpler, less morbid, sultry and languorous than the much praised Study in C sharp minor, opus 25, No. 7. Niecks thinks that this Study "may be counted among Chopin's loveliest compositions . . . it combines classical chasteness of contour with the fragrance of romanticism." Chopin told his faithful pupil, Gutmann, that "he had never in his life written another such melody," and once when hearing it played he raised his arms and cried out: "O ma patrie!"

How well Chopin knew the value of contrast in sentiment and tonality may be observed in the next Study, No. 4. A classic is this piece, which, despite its dark key-color, C sharp minor, as a foil to the preceding one in E, bubbles with life and fairly spurts flame. It recalls the story of the Polish peasantry who are happiest when they sing in the minor mode. The technics of this composition do not lie beneath the surface; they are very much in the way of clumsy fingers and heavy wrists. We wonder why this Study does not figure more frequently in piano recitals. It is a healthy technical test, it is brilliant, and the *coda* is dramatic. Ten bars before the return of the theme there is a stiff digital hedge to jump. The so-called "Black Key" Study No. 5 is familiar and a favorite. It is full of Polish elegance. Von Bülow rather disdainfully speaks of it as a Salon Étude. It is certainly graceful, delicately witty, a trifle naughty, arch, roguish, and delightfully invented. Technically it requires velvet-tipped fingers and a supple wrist. A dark, doleful nocturne is the Study No. 6, in E flat minor. Its melody is full of stifled sorrow. The figure is ingenious and subordinated to the theme. In the E major section the music broadens to dramatic vigor. Chopin was not quite the slave of

his mood. There must be a psychical programme to this Study, some record of a youthful disillusion, but its expression is kept well within continent lines. The Sarmatian composer has not yet unlearned the value of reserve. We emerge into a clearer, a more bracing atmosphere in the C major Study, No. 7. It is a genuine toccata, with moments of tender twilight, withal serving a distinct technical purpose—the study of double-notes changing on one key—and is as sane as the Toccata by Schumann. Here is a brave, an undaunted Chopin, a gay cavalier with the sunshine shimmering about him. There are times when this Study seems like light peeping through the trees in a mysterious forest. With the *delicato* there are Puck-like rustlings, and all the while the pianist is exercising wrists and fingers with a technical exercise. Were ever Beauty and Duty mated so in double-harness? Pegasus pulling a rain-charged cloud over arid land. For study purposes the playing of the entire composition with wrist stroke is advisable; it will secure clear articulation, staccato and finger-memory, also compass more quickly the elusive, flitting character of the piece.

How the F major Study, No. 8, makes the piano sound. What a rich, brilliant sweep it achieves. It elbows the treble to its last euphonious point, glitters and crests itself, only to fall away as if the sea were melodic and could shatter and tumble into tuneful foam. The emotional content is not remarkable, the composition is for the salon or concert hall. At its close one catches the overtones of bustling plaudits and the clapping of gloved palms. Ductility, an aristocratic ease, a delicate touch and fluent technique will carry off this Study with good effect. Technically it is useful—one must speak of the usefulness of Chopin even in these imprisoned irridescent bubbles. A slower *tempo* than the old marking is not amiss, as the Herz and Czerny ideal of velocity vanished with the shallow dip of the keys in Chopin's days—which had much to do with the swiftness and lightness of his playing. The nobler, more sonorous tone of the latter-day concert grand demands greater breadth of style, less speedy passage-work. There can be no doubt as to the wisdom of a broader treatment of this charming display piece. The F minor Study, No. 9, is the first one of his tone studies in which the mood is more petulant than tempestuous. This melody is morbid, almost irritatingly so, and yet not without a certain accent of grandeur. There is a persistency of repetition that foreshadows the Chopin of the later, sadder years. The figure in the left hand is the first in which a prominent part is given that member. Not as noble and sonorous a figure as the one in the C minor Study, it may be viewed as a distinct forerunner to the bass of the D minor Prelude, opus 28, No. 24. The stretch in the F minor Study is the technical object. It is rather awkward for close-knit fingers.

The next Study in A flat, No. 10, is one of the most charming in the series. There is more depth in it than in the G flat and F major Studies, and its effectiveness on the virtuoso side is unquestionable. A savor of the salon is in its perfumed measures, but there are grace, spontaneity and happiness. Chopin must have been as happy as his sensitive nature permitted him when he conceived this vivacious caprice. A musical Corot, if such a comparison be allowed, is the Study No. 11. Its novel design, delicate arabesques—as if the guitar had been dowered with a soul—and the richness and originality of its harmonic scheme, give us pause to ask if Chopin's technical invention is not almost boundless. The harmonization, with the dispersed position of the underlying harmonies, is far more wonderful; but nowadays the chord of the tenth and more remote intervals seem no longer daring; modern composition has devilled the musical alphabet into the caverns of the grotesque; nevertheless, there are harmonies on the last page of this Study that still excite wonder. The fifteenth bar from the end is one that Richard Wagner must have admired, and from that bar to the close every group is masterly. Remember, this Study is a nocturne. It should not be taken at too speedy a *tempo*. The color-scheme is celestial, the ending a sigh, not unmixed with happiness. Chopin had his moments of content. The dizzy *appoggiatura* leaps in the last few bars set the seal of perfection upon this unique composition. Few pianists produce the aerial effect, the swaying of the tone-tendrils abounding in the composition. Yet this exquisite flight into the blue, this nocturne which should be played before sundown, excited the astonishment of Mendelssohn, the perplexity and wrath of Moscheles, and the contempt of Rellstab,

editor of the "Iris," who wrote in that journal in 1834 about the Studies opus 10: "Those who have distorted fingers may put them right by practising these Studies; but those who have not, should not play them, at least, not without a surgeon at hand."

We have now arrived at the last Study in opus 10, the magnificent one in C minor, No. 12. In it the young Polish eagle begins to face the sun, begins to mount on wind-weaving pinions. Four pages suffice for a background upon which the composer has flung with overwhelming fury the darkest, the most demoniacal expressions of his nature. Here no veiled surmise, no smothered rage, but all sweeps along in tornadic passion. Karasowski's story may be true or not regarding the genesis of the work; but true or not, it is one of the greatest dramatic outbursts in the literature of the piano. Powerful in design, pride, force and speed, it never relaxes its grim grip from the first shrill dissonance to the overwhelming chordal close. The end rings out like the crack of creation. It is elemental. Karasowski writes: "Grief, anxiety, despair over the fate of his relations and his dearly beloved father filled the measures of his sufferings." (The fall of Warsaw into the hands of the Russians, alluded to above.) "Under the influence of this mood he wrote the C minor Étude, called the Revolutionary. Out of the mad and tempestuous storm of passages for the left hand the melody arises aloft, now passionate and anon proudly majestic, until thrills of awe stream over the listener, and the image is evoked of Zeus hurling thunderbolts at the world." The Study is full of pathos; it compasses the sublime, and yet in its most torrential moments the composer never loses his intellectual equipoise. It has but one rival in the Chopin Studies—No. 12, opus 25, in the same key.

II

Twelve Studies, opus 25, are dedicated to the Countess d'Agoult, the mother of Liszt's children. The set opens with the familiar study in A flat, so familiar that I shall not make much ado about it except to say that it is delicious, but played often and badly. For Schumann it was an Æolian harp "possessed of all the musical scales." All that modern editing has accomplished for it is to hunt up fresh accentuations, so that the piece is become almost a study in false accents. Chopin, as Schumann has pointed out, did not permit every one of the small notes to be distinctly heard. "It was rather an undulation of the A flat major chord, here and there thrown aloft by the pedal." The twenty-fourth bar is so Lisztian that Liszt must have benefitted by its harmonies.

"And then he played the second in the book, in F minor, one in which his individuality displays itself in a manner never to be forgotten. How charming, how dreamy it was! Soft as the song of

a sleeping child." Schumann wrote this about the study in F minor, opus 25, No. 2, which whispers not of baleful deeds in a dream, as does the last movement of the B flat minor Sonata, but is indeed "the song of a sleeping child." No comparison can be prettier, for there is a sweet, delicate drone that sometimes issues from childish lips possessing a charm for ears attuned to poetry. This must have been the Study that Chopin played for Henrietta Voigt at Leipsic, September 12, 1836. She said: "The overexcitement of his fantastic manner is imparted to the keen-eared. It made me hold my breath. Wonderful is the ease with which his velvet fingers glide, I might say fly, over the keys. He has enraptured me—in a way which hitherto had been unknown to me. What delighted me was the childlike, natural manner which he showed in his demeanor and in his playing." Von Bülow believes that the interpretation of the magical music should be without sentimentality, almost without shading

—clearly, delicately and dreamily executed. "An ideal *pianissimo,* an accentless quality, and completely without passion or *rubato.*" There is little doubt that this was the way Chopin played it. Liszt is an authority on the subject and Georges Mathias corroborates him. It should be played in that Chopin whisper of which Mendelssohn said "that for him nothing more enchanting existed." This Study contains much beauty, and every bar rules over a little harmonic kingdom. It is so lovely that not even the Brahms distortion in double-notes can dull its magnetic crooning. At times its design is so delicate that it recalls the faint, fantastic traceries made by frost on glass. As a Study in mixed rhythms it is valuable. Rubinstein and Annette Essipowa ended it with echo-like effects on the four C's, the pedal floating the tone. Schumann thinks the third study in F major less novel in character, although "here the master showed his admirable bravura powers." It is a spirited caprice with four different voices, if one pulls apart the brightly colored petals of the thematic flower, and thus reveals the chemistry of its delicate growth. "The third voice is the chief one, and after it the first, because they determine the melodic and harmonic contents," writes Kullak. The profile of the melody is in the eighth-notes. They give the meaning to the decorative pattern. And what charm, buoyancy and sweetness there are in this caprice. It has the elusive, tantalizing charm of a humming-bird in flight. The human element is almost eliminated. We are in the open. The sun blazes in the blue. Even when the tone deepens, when the shadows grow cooler and darker in the B major section, there is little hint of sadness. The harmonic shifts are subtle, admirable, the ever-changing devices of the figuration. The fourth study in A minor is a rather sombre, nervous composition, which besides being an Étude also indicates a slightly pathologic condition. With its breath-catching syncopations and narrow emotional range it has its moments of interest if not actual power. Stephen Heller said that this study reminded him of the first bar of the Kyrie—rather the Requiem Æternam of Mozart's Requiem. If not taken at a rapid pace the *cantilena* is heard to better advantage.

It is safe to say that the fifth study in E minor is less often heard in the concert room than any of its companions. Yet it is a sonorous piano piece, rich in embroideries and decorative effect in the middle section. Perhaps the rather perverse, capricious and not too amiable character of the opening page has made pianists wary of playing it in recital. The middle part, with its melody for the thumb and arpeggios, recalls Thalberg. It was Louis Ehlert who wrote of the Study in G sharp minor, No. 6, "Chopin not only versifies an exercise in thirds; he transforms it into such a work of art that in studying it one could sooner fancy himself on Parnassus than at a lesson." And in all piano literature there is no more remarkable example of the merging of matter and manner. The means justifies the end, and the means employed by the composer in this instance are beautiful; beautiful is the word that best describes the architectonics of this study. With the Schumann Toccata, the G sharp minor study stands at the portals of the delectable land of Double-Notes. Both compositions have a common ancestry in the Czerny Toccata. After reading through all the double-note studies for the instrument it is in the nature of a miracle to come upon Chopin's transfiguration of such a barren and mechanical exercise. His study is first music, then a technical problem. Here is not the place to discuss the different fingerings. Each virtuoso has his predilection. What fingering Chopin preferred is aside from the mark, for the action of his piano was easy compared with ours. Von Bülow calls the seventh study in C sharp minor a nocturne, a duo for 'cello and flute. Its dialogue is intimate in feeling. For the contemporaries of Chopin it was one of his greatest efforts. In it are traces of life-weariness. It is both morbid and elegiac. There is nostalgia in its measures, the nostalgia of a sick soul. The D flat Study, No. 8, has been described as the most useful exercise in the whole range of Étude literature. It is an admirable study in double-sixths and is euphonious, even in the passage of consecutive fifths that formerly set theorists at odds. The nimble study that follows, in the key of G flat, No. 9, usually bears the title of "The Butterfly." It is graceful rather than deep and is a prime favorite as an encore piece. It has been compared to a Charles Mayer composition, but the boot is on the other leg. Asiatic in its wildness is the B minor study, No. 10. Its monophonic character recalls the Chorus of Dervishes in Beethoven's "Ruins of Athens." Niecks finds it "a real pandemonium." This Étude is technically an important one. The opening, portentous and sour, becomes a driving whirlwind of tone. There is lushness in the octave melody; the tune may be a little overripe, but it is sweet, sensuous music and about it hovers the hush of a rich evening in early autumn. The close is dramatic.

The canvas of the A minor study, the "Winter Wind," No. 11, is Chopin's largest—thus far—in this opus 25. Not even in the two Concertos is there the resistless overflow of this Étude, which has been justly compared to the screaming of wintry blasts. The theme is never relaxed and its fluctuating harmonic surprises are many. The end is notable for the fact that scales appear: Chopin seldom uses scale-figures in his Studies (and trills sparingly). From Hummel to Herz and Thalberg the keyboard had glittered with spangled scales. Chopin must have been sick of them, as sick as he was of the left-hand melody with arpeggiated figures in the right *à la* Thalberg. In the first C sharp minor Study, opus 10, there is a run for the left hand in the *coda*. In the seventh Study, similar key, opus 25, there are more. The second Study, in A minor, opus 10, is a chromatic scale study; but there are no other specimens in this form till the mighty run at the conclusion of the A minor Study, opus 25, No. 11. Of course, this doesn't apply to the A flat Polonaise, opus 53, or other compositions. The Study in question demands power and endurance. Also passion and no little poetry. It is true storm-music, and the theme in the bass moves throughout in processional splendor. The prime technical difficulty is the management of the thumb, but the didactic side need not concern us here. As for the last Study in opus 25, the C minor, No. 12, I may only add that it is something more than an "exercise in unbroken chord passages for both hands," as has been said. It is grandiose, and there is a primeval, naked simplicity in its tumultuous measures that reveals the puissant soul of Chopin. And /it is eloquent. It is rugged. An epic of the piano, it is far removed from the musical dandyism of the drawing-room. Chopin here is Chopin the Conqueror.

III

In 1840, "Trois nouvelles Études" by Frédéric Chopin appeared in the "Méthode des Méthodes pour le piano par I. Moscheles et F. J. Fétis." Odd company for the Polish composer. "Internal evidence seems to show," says Niecks, "that these weakest of the master's Studies—which, however, are by no means uninteresting and certainly very characteristic—may be regarded, more than opus 25, as the outcome of a gleaning." But the last two decades have contributed much to the artistic stature of these three supplementary Studies (which are sometimes erroneously described as posthumous, though published nine years before the composer's death). They have something of the concision of the Preludes. The first is admirable. In F minor, the theme in triplet quarters, broad, sonorous, passionate, is unequally pitted against eighth-notes in the bass. A rhythmic problem, this, and not difficult to solve. It is the emotional content that attracts. Deeper than the F minor Study in opus 25 is this one, and though the doors never swing wide open we may divine the tragic issues concealed. Beautiful in a different way is the A flat Study that follows; again the problem is a rhythmic one, and again the composer demonstrates his seemingly exhaustless invention, and his power in evoking a single mood, envisaging its lovely contours and letting it melt away as if dream-magic. Replete with gentle sprightliness and lingering sweetness is this Study. Chopin, like Wagner, possesses a hypnotic mastery over his auditors. Don't bother your head over the "triplicity in biplicity" of Kullak, or the pedantry of von Bülow—whose brain was surely compartmentized like an apothecary's shelves. Too many editors spoil the music. In all the editions save one that I have seen, the third Study in D flat begins on A flat, like the popular waltz in D flat. The exception is Klindworth, who starts with B flat, the note above. This Study is flooded with sunny good-humor and arouses the most cheering thoughts. Its technical aim is a simultaneous performance of *legato* and *staccato*. The result is like an idealized Waltz in *allegretto* movement, the incarnation of joy tempered by aristocratic reserve. Chopin never romps, but he jests wittily and always with taste. This Study fitly closes his remarkable labors in the form, and it is as if he had signed it—"F. Chopin *et ego in Arcady*."

Our admiration for the Studies is tinged with wonder at such a prodigal display of thematic and technical invention. Their variety is great, the æsthetic side is never neglected for the mechanical, and in the most poetic of them stuff may be found for delicate as well as heroic fingers. These Studies are exemplary essays in style and emotion. In them all Chopin is mirrored. When most of his piano music has gone the way of things fashioned by mortal hands, these Studies will still endure; will stand for the nineteenth century, as Beethoven crystallized the eighteenth, Bach the seventeenth centuries, in the music of the pianoforte. Chopin is a classic.

James Huneker

Thematic Index.

Douze grandes Études.

À F. LISZT.

F. CHOPIN. Op. 10, № 1.

Étude.

F. CHOPIN. Op. 10, Nº 2.

Étude.

F. CHOPIN. Op. 10, № 3.

Étude.

F. CHOPIN. Op. 10, Nº 4.

Étude.

F. CHOPIN. Op.10, № 5.

Étude.

F. CHOPIN. Op. 10, Nº 6.

Douze grandes Études.

Vivace. (♩.= 84.)

F. CHOPIN. Op. 10, № 7.

7.

Etude.

F. CHOPIN. Op. 10, № 8.

Étude.

F. CHOPIN. Op. 10, № 9

Étude.

F. CHOPIN. Op. 10, № 10.

Étude.

F. CHOPIN. Op. 10, № 11.

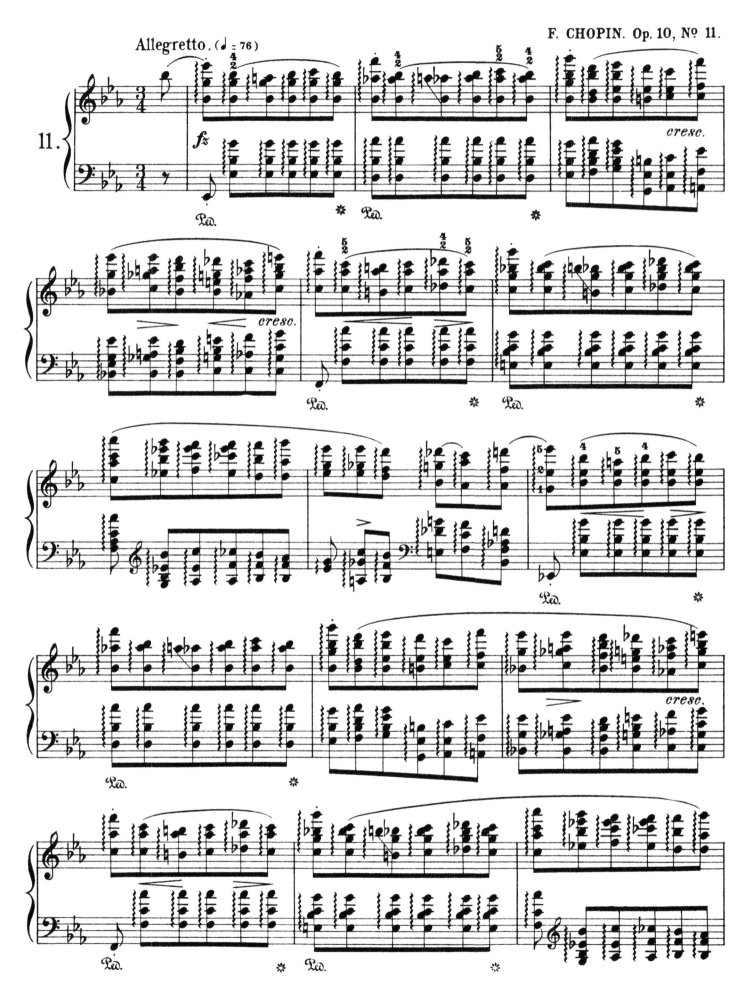

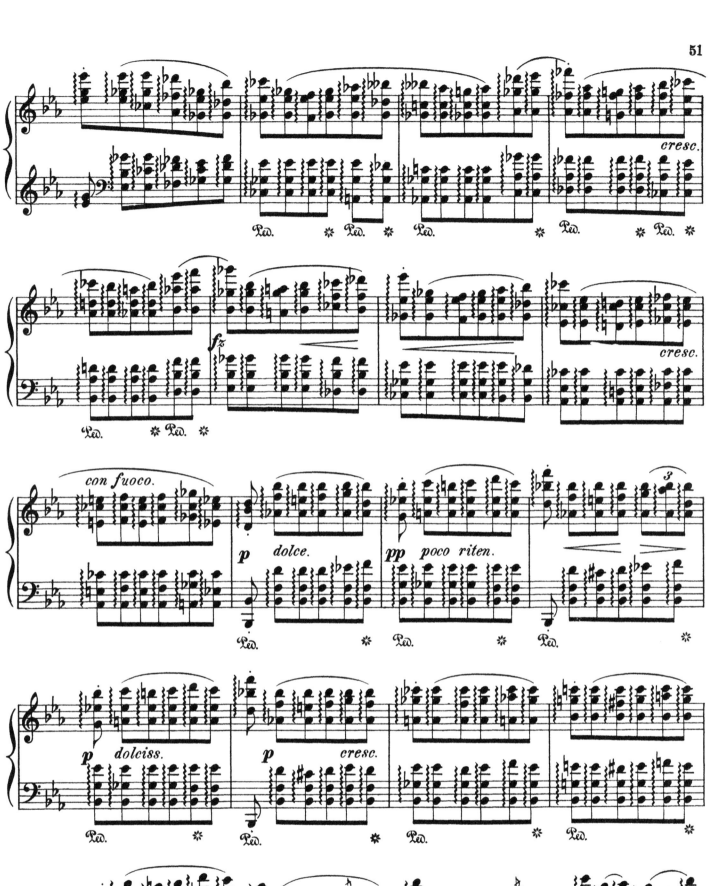

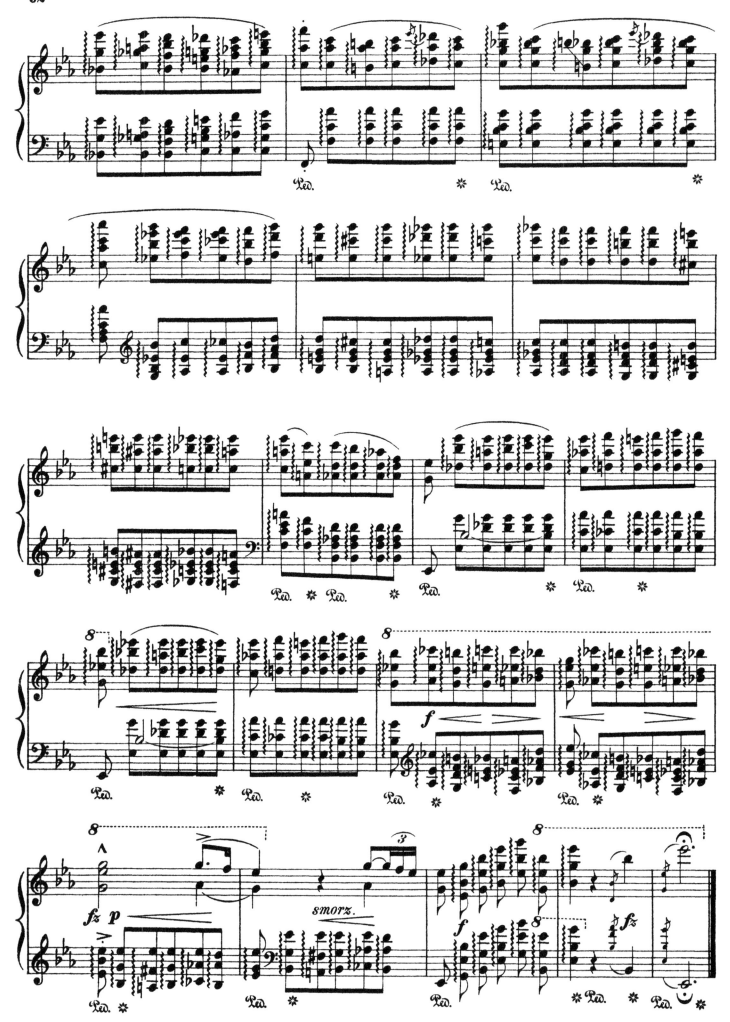

Étude.

Allegro con fuoco. (♩ = 160.)

F. CHOPIN. Op. 10, № 12.

Douze Études.

à Mme la Comtesse d'AGOULT.

F. CHOPIN. Op. 25, N.º 1.

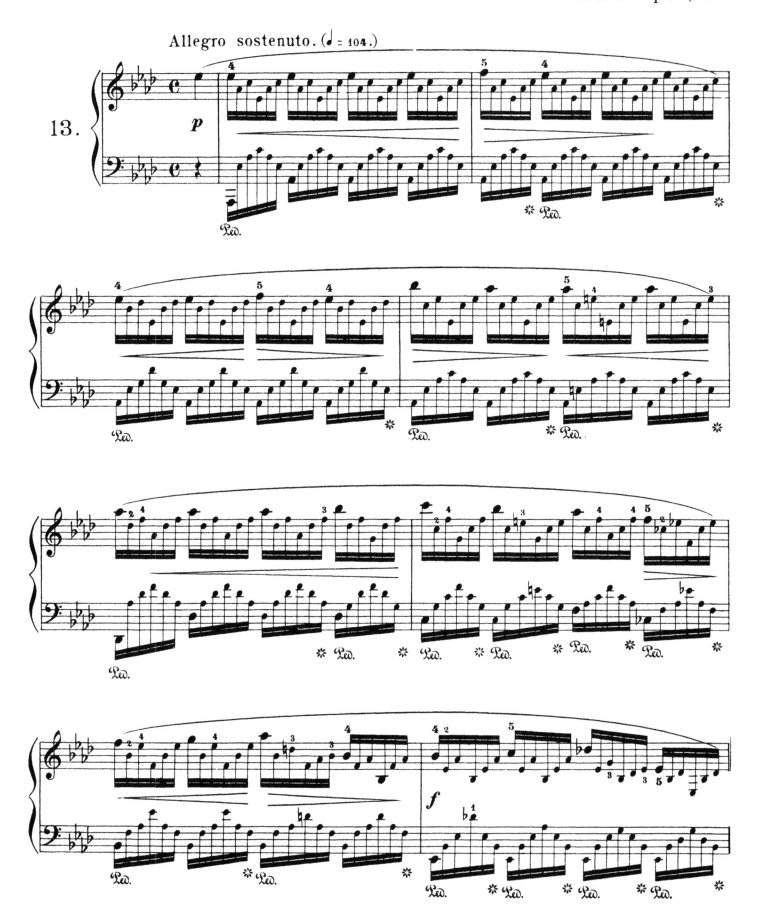

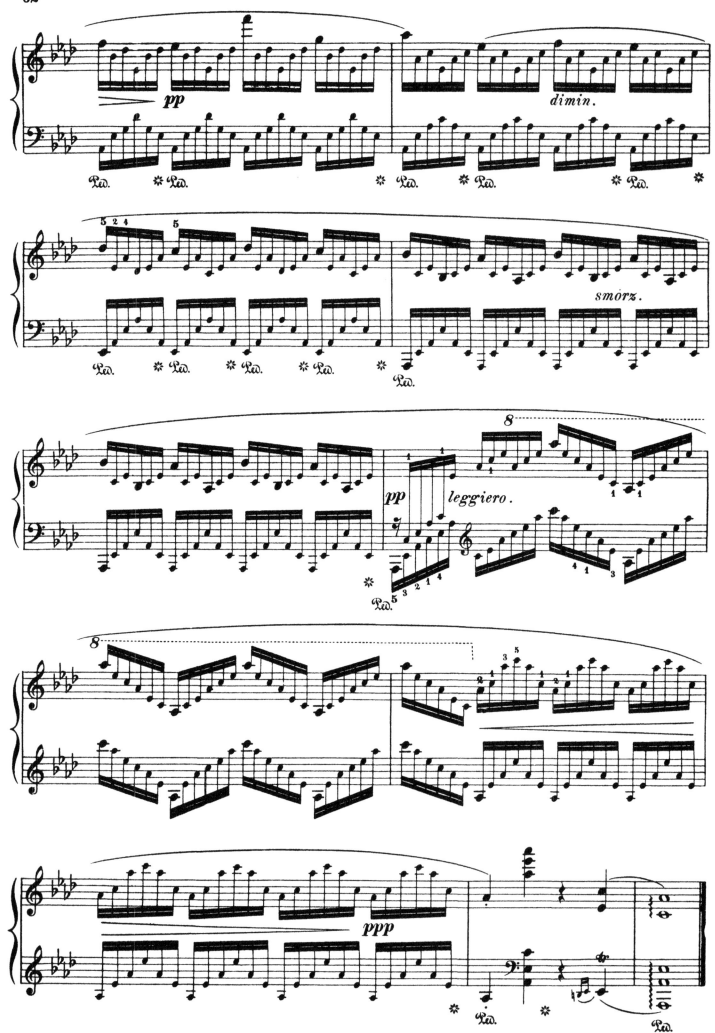

Étude.

F. CHOPIN. Op. 25, № 2.

Presto. (♩ = 112.)

14.

Étude.

Allegro. (♩ = 120.)

F. CHOPIN. Op. 25, № 3.

15.

leggiero.

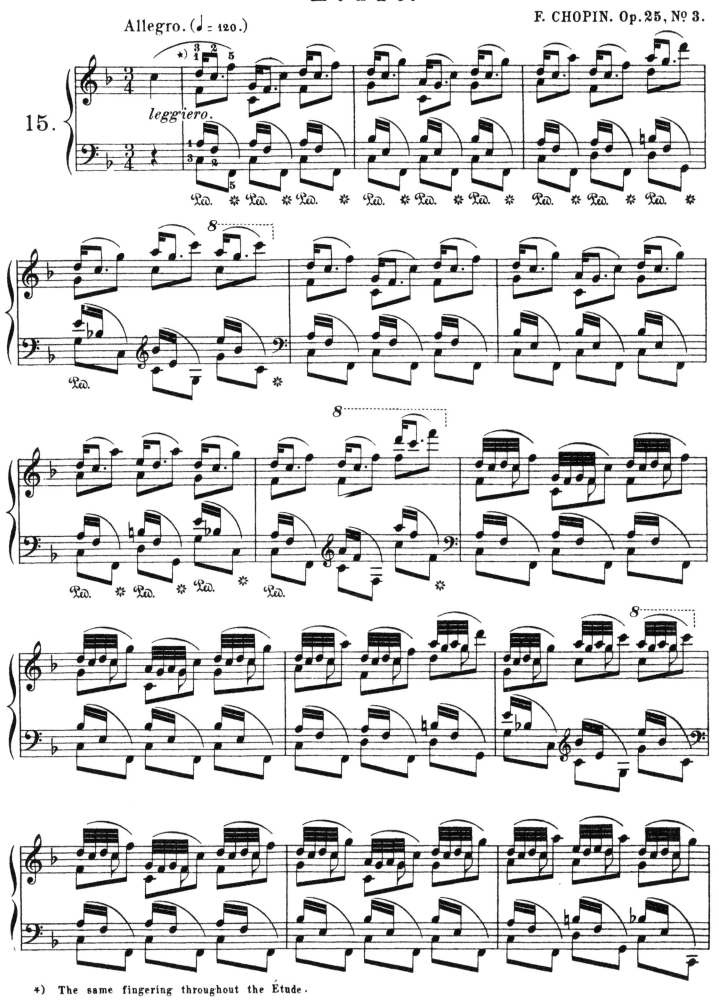

*) The same fingering throughout the Étude.

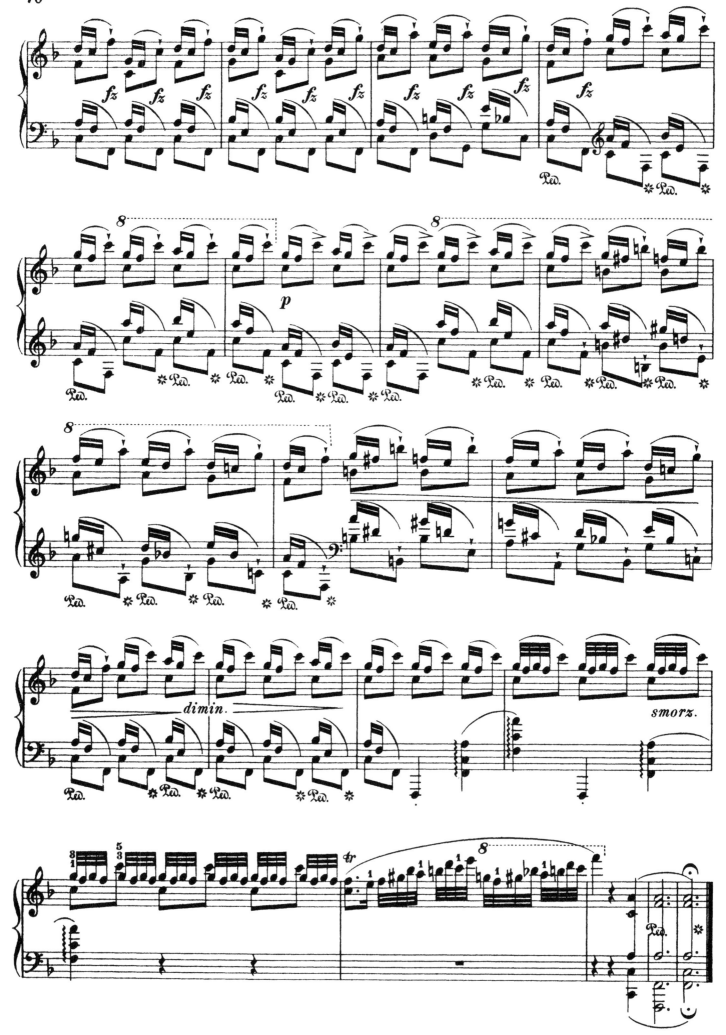

Étude.

F. CHOPIN. Op. 25, № 4.

Agitato. ($\quad$ = 120.)

16.

Étude.

F. CHOPIN. Op. 25, № 5.

17.

N.B. The appoggiaturas are to be executed like those written out in full at the beginning of the Étude, except that the upper notes are sustained

Étude.

Allegro. (♩ = 69.)

F. CHOPIN. Op. 25, № 6.

18.

sotto voce.

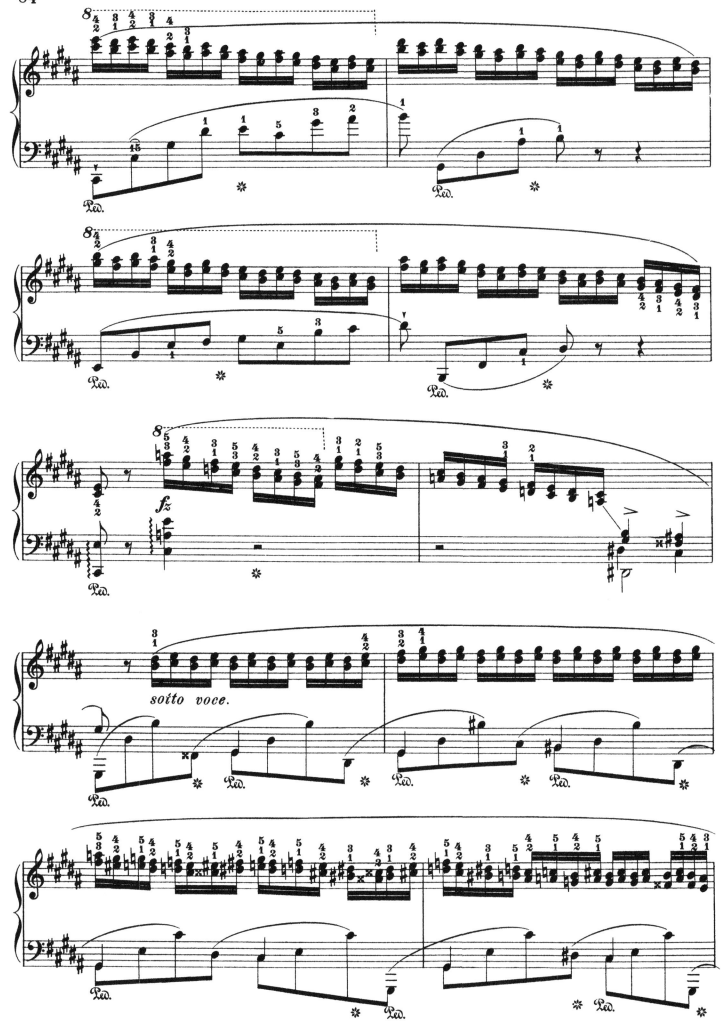

Douze Études.

F. CHOPIN. Op. 25, Nº 7.

Étude.

F. CHOPIN. Op. 25, No 8.

Vivace legato. (♩ = 69.)

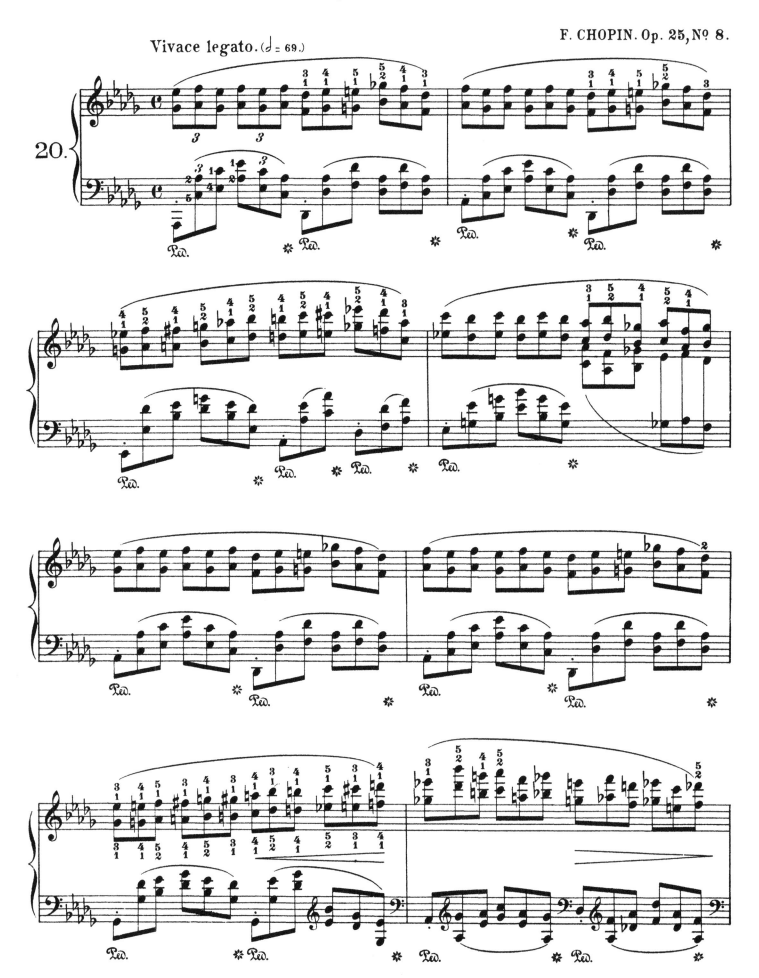

Étude.

F. CHOPIN. Op. 25, № 9.

Étude.

F. CHOPIN. Op. 25, № 10.

Allegro con fuoco. (♩ = 72.)

Tempo I.

Étude.

F. CHOPIN. Op. 25, № 11.

23.

Étude.

Allegro molto, con fuoco. (♩=80.)

F. CHOPIN. Op, 25. № 12.

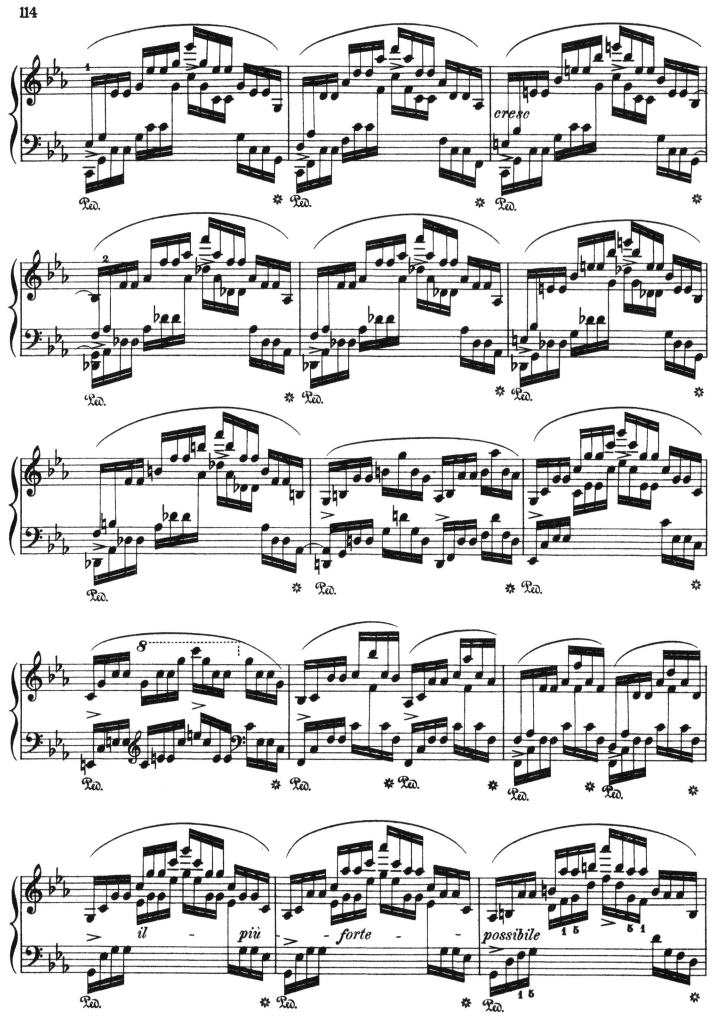

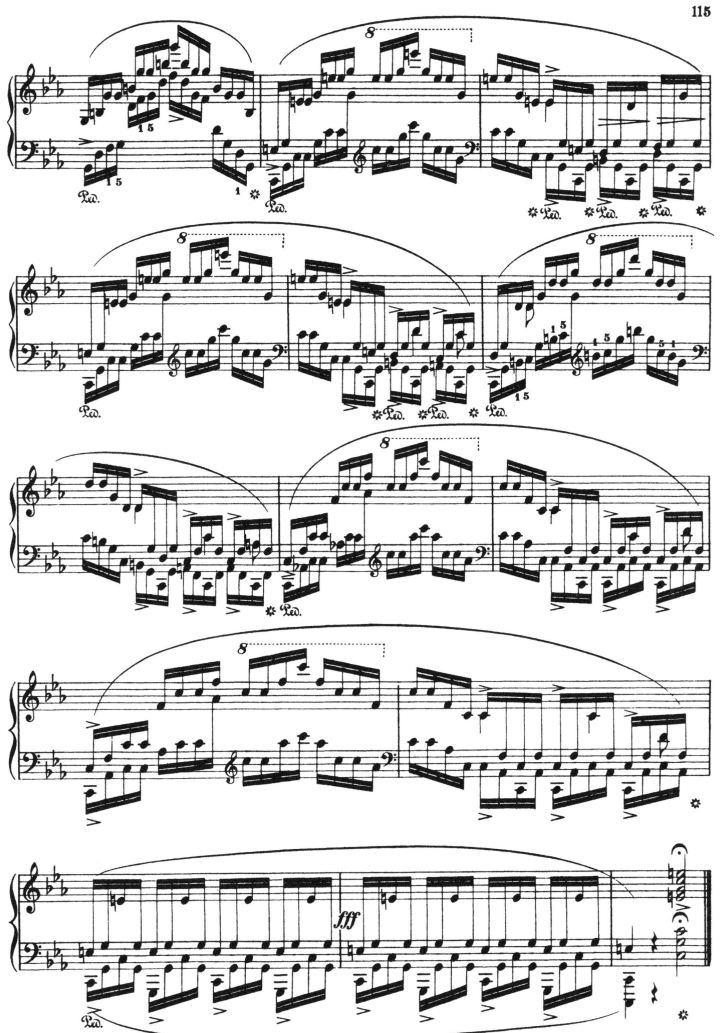

Trois Études.
(Composées pour la Méthode de Moscheles & Fétis.)
Nº 1.

Andantino.

F. CHOPIN.

Trois Études.

(Composeés pour la Méthode de Moscheles & Fétis.)

N.º 2.

F. CHOPIN.

Trois Études.

Composées pour la Méthode de Moscheles & Fétis.

Nᵒ 3.

F. CHOPIN.